CONTENTS

Raspberry Kingdom

by
Renée Hermanson

THE UPPER ROOM
Nashville, Tennessee

RASPBERRY KINGDOM
Copyright © 1978 by The Upper Room

The quotation from "The Road Not Taken" is from *The Poetry of Robert Frost*
edited by Edward Connery Lathem. Copyright 1916, © 1969 by Holt, Rinehart
and Winston. Copyright 1944 by Robert Frost. Reprinted by permission of Holt,
Rinehart and Winston, Publishers.

Quotations from *Markings* by Dag Hammarskjöld, translated by Leif Sjöberg and W.
H. Auden and copyright © 1964 by Alfred A. Knopf, Inc., and Faber and Faber,
Ltd., are used with the permission of the publisher, Alfred A. Knopf, Inc.

Design and illustrations by Pat Van Atta

First Printing, August, 1978 (8)
Second Printing, April, 1980 (5)

Library of Congress Catalog Card Number: 78-62985
ISBN 0-8358-0374-0
Printed in the United States of America

PREFACE

"What is your book about?" friends ask me when I am brave enough to tell them why my typewriter is clicking instead of my knitting needles or sewing machine.

"Well . . . it is . . . a book about picking raspberries."

"A nature book?" They look puzzled. Anyone to whom I would confide my secret must wonder at that. They would also know that I am a student of ideas and actions, not botany.

"Not exactly. It is a book of reflections on life as I saw it in the raspberry patch."

"Oh."

To all my puzzled friends, to readers who think the book is on the wrong shelf, and to editors who also feel that a book should be "about" something, I offer this explanation. When I followed the path of most resistance into the raspberry patch, it was only because of my mother-in-law's enthusiasm for berry picking. My first excursions were discouraging; I am not a nature child. But the fruit I picked was delicious, and I found in those hours a seclusion I could find nowhere else. Brought to the picking by another's excitement, kept there by my own love for fresh fruit, I gradually became aware of the less tangible fruit, the opportunity for solitude and contemplation. As I picked, I took notes from nature and saw in each day's work a parable of life. I have shared my fruit with family and friends; now I am ready to share the other part, lessons I am convinced were taught by the Lord of love in an unusual school.

Good news sharing is like that. We are drawn to it by someone else's testimony, and because of their promises we stick with it even if it proves disappointing at first. Some of our motives may be selfish, and we may not share the experience in the same way, but if our venture is based on truth, we will find meaning of our own in it. And then we will have our own good news to share, our own experience to reinforce the reality of that news.

That, then, is what this book is about. That is also what witnessing is about—listening, accepting, living, experiencing, sharing. Jesus said, "I will make you [pickers] of men."

Earth's crammed with heaven,
And every common bush afire with God;
But only he who sees
takes off his shoes;
The rest sit round it
and pluck blackberries. [1]

ELIZABETH BARRETT BROWNING

1. I'M NOT THE TYPE

"What's a smart city girl like you doing in a place like this?" is the question I kept asking myself that first day in the raspberry patch. I had threaded my way through the jungle of skyscrapers in San Francisco when I was fourteen and since then had competed on this nation's freeways and successfully dodged racing taxis and buses all over the world. I don't remember feeling quite so threatened by any of that as I did in the tangle of brush just across the road from our newly built cabin in Minnesota's north country.

I tried to recall Grandma's rave notices on berry picking. She was at home among the raspberry canes, remembering her childhood. I had no such history. My only contact with country living had been a summer week spent on my aunt's farm, during which time I fell off a horse (while it was standing still) and angered my uncle by being too timid to coax the cows home for milking. Perhaps those experiences had made their mark on me; stamped me with some deep defensiveness against the simple life.

I remembered my oldest son's introduction to farm animals. He loved his farm picture books and was excited about seeing real cows and pigs and chickens, but neither of us had realized how different those miniature, friendly beasts in the books were from the real thing.

"They're so *big!*" he whispered as he held tightly to my hand.

The raspberry patch was not "so big," but it was certainly a far cry from all the stories I had read about people running through fields of wild flowers, lying in grassy meadows, and strolling through deep forest glades. Those stories failed to point out that grass and brush scratch exposed skin and that an unbelievable percentage of branches grow exactly at eye level. There was no mention of the caution necessary to avoid falling through rotten timber or stumbling into a swarm of bees. Nothing at all about flies or mosquitoes. What, I wondered, is so great about this?

Grandma feels the same way about a strange city. To her it seems raucous and untamed, threatening. We could move, as aliens, into each other's domain, but we could not be immediately at home. We needed time to explore and examine, time to desensitize ourselves to what was irritating and to sensitize ourselves to the beauty and value of each place.

I made many excursions into the raspberry patch wondering why I bothered at all, muttering temperate oaths to myself, thinking how much pleasanter it would be sunning myself on the dock or reading a book in the comfort of the rocker in the cabin. I went into the business of picking raspberries "kicking and struggling," as C. S. Lewis says, with only a fragment of my will engaged in it. But it was the fragment that was responsible for getting me there. The rest of me could be at odds with the whole situation, but that one part that counted got me across the road and up the bank into the woods.

Some of us come to Christ in the same way, arguing and dissenting about almost everything. But once that part of us that counts (what some people call our "will") says yes, we are committed, and we go on, as I did in the raspberry patch, questioning and objecting, but continuing. There are those who can throw themselves at the Master's feet with wholehearted abandon and be immediately at home in their new environment. Others of us must fight the battle every inch of the way, gaining ground gradually, fearfully clutching the one slim cord that ties us to him.

Jane Merchant wrote movingly of her battle with pain and discouragement, of times when she cried out, "I can't go on," and then acknowledged that what went on when she could not was God. I'm not sure what kept me going back to the raspberries, but I know what keeps me going back to God. It is his "love that will not let me go," his patient leading that brings me along the path and welcomes me into his kingdom.

> Nature sides with grace. We are pressed from above by grace and from below by nature. We are squeezed into the Kingdom. . . . When you say Yes to Jesus Christ, the universe says Yes to you.[2]
>
> E. STANLEY JONES

One-half of knowing what you want
is knowing what you must give up
before you get it.

SIDNEY HOWARD

2. THE OTHER HALF

My lessons in the raspberry patch were conceived in wariness and birthed in struggle. I learned after the first day that proper attire had nothing to do with fashion. The keynote was protection, from the scratching brush and ravenous mosquitoes. That meant covering up everything possible. On my first trip, I had swung gaily into the adventure wearing shorts and a sleeveless blouse (it was, after all, a very warm day). That tour was short-lived. From then on, I decided that protection came before pride. I wore long pants (old ones, that didn't mind snags and green stains), stockings, a long-sleeved shirt, and scarf or hat. If I looked like I had been put together in the bargain department of the Salvation Army store, it didn't matter. The dress had to fit the game.

Somewhat encumbered with all that covering, I found it best to go picking early in the morning, before the sun rose to its most generous height. That meant another sacrifice, giving up those luxurious, lazy mornings in bed. It was a war between bed and berries, and they took turns winning.

Fresh berries for my breakfast was often the only goal of my foraging. And I found myself willing to sacrifice my vanity, my sleep, my comfort for that meager prize. There was no way I could get the fruit on my own terms, without bugs or humid discomfort, at a more convenient time of day. If I wanted them, I had to meet nature more than half way.

Many things have come easily for me and my generation. Our parents and grandparents tell us we don't know what work is or what hunger and hardship are all about. And we really don't want to know. It is not something most of us go searching for. But every so often there is some little challenge that rouses us to make what we consider a "sacrifice." When I want to lose weight, I need to say no to the tempting piece of cake or pizza. If I really want to write a book, I must tear myself away from someone else's book, or the TV, and get away to my corner to work. My pledge to a continuing education demands fewer shopping trips and coffee klatches and more time spent in classes and libraries. If I really wanted those raspberries, I had to be willing to give up a little.

As a member of the "soft" generation, this does not come easily. I fuss when it is too hot or too cold, when the traffic doesn't move to suit me, when things don't fall into place automatically. I fret because life doesn't always operate according to my schedule. Then, in some moment of illumination, I understand that I must meet life on its terms. That in order to wring anything out of it, I must be willing to do some sacrificing and struggling. My marriage won't be successful because I say I want it that way. I won't be a good mother simply because I decide it should be so. I may want to climb a mountain "because it's there," but I won't get far unless I also decide that I am willing to submit myself to the rigors of weather and physical stress.

Getting into God's kingdom is, in some ways, the easiest task in the world. All we have to do is say yes to his offer. But saying that yes is also the hardest thing for most of us. Because the other side of that yes says no to our own selfish will. It turns its back on our vanity, on the way we think things should be done.

Oswald Chambers explains it this way, "After we have been perfectly related to God in sanctification, our faith has to be worked out in actualities. We shall be scattered . . . into inner desolations and made to know what internal death to God's blessings means, . . . [where God] is pointing out that we have not been interested in Himself but only in His blessings." [3]

What we need, he concludes, is "spiritual grit," the kind that is given only by the Author of all spiritual gifts. Our task is to accept it.

*When I hear somebody sigh
that "Life is hard,"
I am always tempted to ask,
"Compared to what?"*
SYDNEY HARRIS

3. THE ROAD TO REAL

Sometimes I thought my excursions into the woods had a masochistic bent. Other people plunged into that wilderness with cheerful abandon, unaware of the discomfort of heat and insects, but not me. I was continually aware of them and of the sacrifices I was making to pick berries.

What made me do it? Was it akin to the urge that makes people climb icy mountains or take safaris into steamy jungles? My adventure was not nearly so grand, but I found I had two things in common with those who dared such things. One was purely material—I wanted those raspberries. Tangible rewards often are enough to lure us from security and comfort. The desire for money, power, and recognition has driven any number of people to dare and to sacrifice beyond their own sense of proportion.

The second was more subtle. It was an inward drive I could not clearly define or understand but which implied that I would be rewarded for my efforts by something that would remain after the last raspberry had been scraped from the bowl. These wisps of promise buzzed in the hum of insects and rustle of trees, they mumbled in the cracking of broken branches and

sang in the carols of birds. Although I couldn't
understand the words, they beckoned me back again
and again, like the Siren's song, to leave comfort and
pleasure behind for something more—something
unspoken, unspeakable.

Solitude and the lack of interruption was the first
reward. After twenty years of living with no time by
myself, this experience sent me into environmental
shock. I talked out loud to myself. But before long I fell
under the spell of aloneness and I began to crave it.
Although I have difficulty being serious about talking to
my plants at home, I had no trouble at all conversing
with the raspberry canes, the thistles, bees, and
mosquitoes I met in the woods. I was only a few steps
across the road from our cabin, where people talked to
people and bees and flies were an intrusion. But in that
short space, through the hedge of bushes, I moved into
a separate world. I began to understand how astronauts
could survive the restrictive immobility of their space
capsules. In that world beyond our world, in that
breathless expanse of space, physical discomfort may
pale and retire to a subconscious level. But then again,
it may not. Space explorers may be continually irritated
by the cramped quarters, the clumsy clothing, and
liquid diet, but nevertheless endure it for the sake of
the experience. They are responding to a call that holds
infinite promise.

We once hiked down a steep, rocky trail into the
Grand Canyon, for no more reason than to say we had
done it and, I guess, because "it was there." We went

only one fourth of a mile down from the top, but with switchbacks along the edge of the canyon wall, the actual walking distance was much longer and the grade was achingly tiresome. Once down, there was nothing to do but return to the top, no matter how torturous the climb. As I struggled along the path on the return trip, I thought of the satisfaction I would have in telling of this adventure when I returned home. It would give me something to "drop" when the conversation lagged at some future dinner party.

But when I finally inched my way over the last ridge of rock and stood to look back down the stony trail leading into the depths of the canyon, I wasn't thinking of telling anybody anything. I was filled with awe at what I had just experienced and exhilarated with the pure satisfaction of having done it.

We sometimes get very intellectual and pragmatic about our efforts, laying plans and making decisions. We resist any impulse that could upset our designs. The apostle Paul, in spite of his strict Hebrew theological training, had no such inhibitions. They had all been abandoned in the dust of a road outside Damascus. He claimed no distinction because of his efforts in spreading the gospel; he was "under orders," driven by divine compulsion. Beatings, hardships, and arrests were not discounted (in fact, he must have counted them; he said he had more than anyone else!), but they did not deter him because he was following the path laid out for him by the Everlasting One. To answer that voice can mean for us, as it did for Paul, the discovery of a new promised land. And afterward, when we go back to our other world, where people hear only each other, we no longer wonder which one of them is real and true. We know the truth and we are free.

"[Being real] doesn't happen all at once," said the Skin Horse.

"You become. It takes a long time. That's why it doesn't often happen to people who break easily, or have sharp edges, or who have to be carefully kept. Generally, by the time you are Real, most of your hair has been loved off, and your eyes drop out and you get loose in the joints and very shabby. But these things don't matter at all, because once you are Real you can't be ugly . . . [and] you can't become unreal again. It lasts for always."[4]

MARGERY WILLIAMS

'Tis ye, 'tis your estrangèd faces,
That miss the many-splendored thing. [5]

FRANCIS THOMPSON

4. TREASURE HUNT

Once I was past the arguments with myself over whether to pick or not to pick and at last having decided to endure the discomfort of it all, I began to establish a pattern in my activities. Treasure hunting was a part of every day's forage. I learned where to look for the best berries and how to reach them. I also learned that some of the same principles govern the detection of life's treasures. One of the most obvious and yet the most profound is that they are usually concealed.

For centuries people have found it necessary to hide their wealth from other people's greed, sometimes going to great length to assure its safety. Chests of booty and gold were stored in pirate caves, kings' fortunes were hoarded in secret mausoleums. Intrigue surrounded the choice of locations, and lives were lost in the interest of security. I had visited the ancient tombs of Egypt, and while I marveled at the ingenuity exercised in the determination to preserve their wealth, I was struck by the futility of it all. The greatest share of the treasure had been looted; much of what remained had rotted and crumbled, enjoyed, not by the pharaoh in eternal rest, but by archeologists and tourists like myself.

There are other treasures, intangible ones, that remain hidden and useless unless we seek them out. Jesus spoke in parables to hide the truth from his audiences. For what reason? Didn't he want them to know the truth? Or was his storytelling a wry, manipulative gesture designed to make his hearers beg for explanations?

I thought about that as I discovered that many of the loveliest berries were found hidden under the shelter of green foliage. There they were protected from hungry birds who chose their fare indiscriminately and from the heat of the high noon sun, basking instead in the gentler rays that filter through the brush at either end of the day. There they had a chance to grow and ripen, fed by the warmth and moisture of their environment. The only danger in their being sheltered so was that they might remain undiscovered. They might remain there like hidden treasure until their time ran out and there was nothing left but shriveled, useless fruit.

I think there must be truths that suffer the same fate. "There is nothing new under the sun," says the writer of Ecclesiastes. Someone else has observed that there is no such thing as a "new" discovery; we only let what is already true become available to us. Therefore, when a Newton or Curie or Einstein "discovers" something, he or she is merely uncovering a treasure that has been awaiting detection.

These truths are not revealed to the casual passerby. The berries on the underside of the leaves are not found without some effort. People who didn't care enough to

question never understood Jesus' figurative stories.
Something worth finding is worth looking for. The
dilettante will find only green leaves and quaint
Hebrew folk tales.

Occasionally I would decide to browse the bushes
close to the road or spend just a few minutes at the
edge of the thicket, but then the harvest was pitifully
lean. I remembered Jesus' encounter with the wealthy
young man who thought he had all the answers. He
wanted to reap his reward by walking along the road,
without going into the thicket, without facing the
difficulties or seeking out the real treasure. Jesus'
demand that he give up all he had was not only a
demand for sacrifice, but a counsel that he needed to go
deeper into himself to see his real needs. He needed to
dig to find that treasure of truth. It was not to be found
on the surface of laws and rules.

Jesus said, "*Seek* and you will find." That means that
we must look for what he has buried, look beyond our
self-centeredness, our pride, and our willfulness. His
treasure is hidden to prevent the person who is
unwilling to do this from finding it. There are so many
who pass it by, who never bother to look. It is so
precious that it cannot be left out for grabbing by
unthinking people. It is kept secure for those who will
take the time to seek it in faith, for those who will
savor its full flavor.

When I brought my berries back to share with the
family for breakfast, it was often disappointing to watch
them gulp them down without attention to their

perfection. I was disappointed, not only because I felt much of my effort was wasted (were they really tasting them?), but because I knew that they were missing so much of the real flavor, the true beauty that I knew so intimately.

God doesn't make things difficult for us in a capricious or arbitrary way. He acts by design, purposefully. His hidden treasures are meant to be found. He knows our needs. He knows that we must seek in order to realize the value of his riches and that we must ask in order to receive the full realization of the wealth he has to offer.

> Miracles . . . rest not so much upon faces or voices or healing power coming suddenly near to us from afar off, but upon our perceptions being made finer, so that for a moment our eyes can see and our ears can hear what is there about us always.[6]
>
> WILLA CATHER

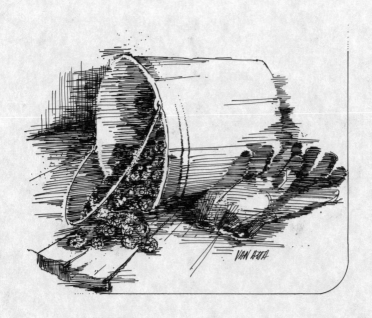

It is not enough to be busy;
so are the ants.
The question is:
What are we busy about?

HENRY DAVID THOREAU

5. A POCKETFUL OF TIME

There are points in my life when an hour is as precious as money in my wallet. When the days are too short and the calendar is pockmarked with notations of meetings, appointments, and deadlines, I wish there were a way to buy an extra hour or two. Then I look at my children and remember how slowly time moved for me once. It had no value then; there was too much of it. Like the prodigal son who spent his fortune as if there were no end to it, my time was spent wastefully, as if it would go on forever.

One definition of *spend* is "to exhaust, to use up, to squander." Youth might be excused for a little squandering, but the Puritan ethic that motivates many of us doesn't tolerate that kind of waste in mature persons. It demands its pound of flesh for every minute of the day—no dawdling, no dreaming, no wasting. That philosophy looks at time as meant for "worthwhile" work, for having physical and mental energies engaged in activity. I think that is one reason I was willing to forsake the less arduous vacation activities in order to pick raspberries. I had relatively little to do in terms of chores at the lake. Housekeeping was reduced to its lowest form, and meals were limited to the simple fare that could be created from three weeks' worth of rations on the cupboard shelves. With no phone, no meetings, or work schedule demands, I had a lot of time to "spend."

But my conscience would not let me spend all that extra time in self-indulgent relaxation. When I tried, the trees whispered, the waves chided, "Why aren't you *doing* something?" Raspberry picking became a task to quiet those accusing voices. If I picked berries in the morning, I could still the chirping cricket of conscience and enjoy the luxury of doing nothing in the afternoon.

But there was another dimension to the "work" I did in the raspberry patch. My investment of time in that work was not only in what I did with my hands. The validity of that kind of work is limited; it is good but not complete. It needs more to round it out, to give it meaning. Along with work, whether it comes simultaneously or apart from the activity, there must be time, I discovered, for contemplation and reflection, for fitting the pieces together. Much of my time in the woods was invested in that kind of mental activity, not all of it valuable. I cannot claim to have given long, uninterrupted hours to deep, significant contemplation. A lot of my mental activity was as wanton and meaningless as much of my feverish busyness. But I learned that physical labor and mental employment complement each other. In my raspberry kingdom my body was struggling with nature's vexations, but my mind was awakened to her delights. Alone on the dock or relaxed in the water, with my body in repose, my mind wrestled with the tireless grey angels of question and doubt. Neither use of time was wasteful. Both were strong threads woven into my view of life, a warp that laid foundations of judgments and decisions and a weft that furnished a sense of oneness with God and all his creatures.

We are not equally endowed with riches to spend or to invest, in either time or money. But each of us has been given some measure of time, a fortune if we see it that way. Each coin in that fortune is precious, for it is the real sum of all we have to spend or give away.

> . . . seeing that you have to do more than have time, save time, kill time; that flowers have an action and that you can be as well as become, can measure depth as well as space, and that it is not enough to take an idiot around the world at four hundred miles an hour if he remains the same idiot when you bring him back to Main Street.[7]
>
> MERIDEL LE SUEUR

There is a tide in the affairs of men,
Which, taken at the flood, leads on to fortune;
Omitted, all the voyage of their life
Is bound in shallows and in miseries. [8]

WILLIAM SHAKESPEARE

6. THE COST

After learning to pay the price of giving up my sleep,
my comfort, and my appearance for the sake of a pailful
of berries, I discovered there was another "hidden
charge" on the price tag. Once in the thick of the
brush, there were scores of bright red berries to choose
from, but the choicest ones, the ones really worth the
effort, were always the hardest to reach.

As I worked my way along the trail of broken
branches that marked another's efforts, I picked what
they had left, or what had ripened since they had been
through the woods. Then, in a dense tangle of canes
and thistles, I often saw a cane laden with oversized,
red-ripe fruit. I climbed over logs, inched between
strong sapling branches and under brittle limbs. I
dodged thistles and fell through rotten piles of
timber—all for two or three perfect raspberries.

Was it madness? Not in that world. In that kingdom
those few berries were worth far more than the current
market price. In my other world, I wouldn't have
fought crowds in the supermarket for a whole box of
berries, but in the woods my priorities changed. When
I compared what was available on the easy path to what
I could have with a little more exertion, I was

compelled to take the more difficult way. A glimpse of excellence made mediocrity intolerable.

Someone said that a culture can be measured by what it stands in line for. Because I hate standing in line, I think that must be a valid assumption. Only the desire for something really worthwhile or the need for something absolutely necessary can force me to spend my time in that way. It is symbolic of the ultimate struggle for me to stand around with nothing to *do*. I was happier in the woods when I could fight my way through nature's fences that I am waiting in a civilized queue.

A few perfect berries in the woods cost me more in time and trial than I would have paid for a quart at the store in town, even if I had had to stand in line. Perhaps it was worth it because the relation between the object of my desire and my own efforts toward achieving it were so obvious and direct. There was no long line of succession between my preparation to work, my working, my earning, and my spending. No tiresome time lags between learning the alphabet and principles of arithmetic and the awarding of a diploma. It was right there; I could see the goal as I labored, almost within reach, seldom unattainable. The promise of those prizes to pick was so real, I could feel and taste the berry before I reached to pull if off the stem.

As a middle-class white American female, I go through life on a well-worn path, following convention in matters of dress and habits, speech and life style. Sometimes it seems easiest to follow the trail others have left, taking from life the meager fruits of their labors. But, praise God, there are occasional glimpses of brighter fruits to tempt me from conformity.

I see in the life of another such radiance and wholeness, I am compelled to succumb to the rigors of disciplined living to find the secret of such a life. I discover in a book the exciting adventures available to a mind willing to learn and I am able to give up some spectator activities in favor of sterner and stricter, but far more rewarding, business. I see through the narrow gate of submission the glories of heaven and the joys of eternal communion with the Lord of lords and I can no longer walk along the wide road of my own self-indulgence.

The promise of reward for obedience and submission can be reason enough to endure the necessary hardships. The struggle itself can bring satisfaction, but either is only half the reward. Getting caught up in the challenges of living the more demanding way is losing the prize. How many people, when the labor is done, suffer a sense of loss and disillusionment? Was the goal not worth it? Was the work more fulfilling than the paycheck?

Not so for the Christian. We can have the best of both worlds. When I obey the command of my Lord to come and partake of his life and death, I am also invited to the celebration of his resurrection. I hear the promise of a new spirit within me and see the vision of life in the new Jerusalem and I know I will not be disappointed. Christ is mine in labor and in rest, and I will know pure joy in him, now and forevermore.

> [Luther's] experience taught him that this grace had cost
> him his very life, and must continue to cost him the
> same price day by day. So far from dispensing him from
> discipleship, this grace only made him a more earnest
> disciple.[9]

DIETRICH BONHOEFFER

*Abraham comes
down from the mountain with Issac
just as he went up,
but the whole situation has changed.*[10]

DIETRICH BONHOEFFER

7. LOOK BACK!

As a stranger in the woods, I was not very systematic in my foraging. I might start out with the intent to cover a certain section of the berry patch, but once in the thick of the brush, I either lost my sense of direction or let myself be led from bush to bush by the lure of bright red splashes on farther canes. When I took a moment to rest or get my bearings, I often looked back and saw a wealth of fruit I had just passed. How could I have missed that? Why didn't I see it as I went by?

I had a teacher once who claimed that life was all a matter of point of view, a sort of life-is-as-you-see-it philosophy. Some people see life only in what is ahead, some only in what is present, and others only in the past. There may be arguments for each viewpoint but not to the exclusion of the others. Living life only for the future loses the gift of the moment and a sense of identity with the riches of the past. When Paul said he pressed on, forgetting what was past, he meant that he did not carry his past as a burden. It did not haunt him. He was free of the guilt of his old ways, but he also acknowledged that he was living on some of the foundations of his past—his knowledge of the scripture from his Hebrew teachers, his mobility and freedom to speak from his Roman citizenship, and his experience as a leader in the Pharisaic community. He also used his past as a point of comparison, as a measure of the change that Christ had brought into his life. The guilt was gone but the reality of his past was not.

I have a journal in which I write with fair regularity—not great prose, but some of my day-to-day experiences and feelings. I have found it helpful in keeping my perspective, in seeing the truth of today and tomorrow. When we get on the other side of something, we see it differently. I can read my journal and relive and experience an answered prayer. I can look back and see how some of my anxieties were unfounded, how they were taken care of when I gave them in trust to the Father, who knows how to give perfect gifts to his children. I don't review it to live in the past or revel in the "good old days," but only to see how far I have come and sometimes to see something I missed the first time.

Remembering again my puny assault on the Grand Canyon's immensity, I thought of how often, when the climb back up seemed impossible, I sought reassurance by looking back to see how far I had come. Somehow the distance was easier charted that way. It looked so far to the top and yet, measured by the length already managed, it was not unattainable.

When I look back to beginnings, to the ultimate genesis, I am reminded that I came from dust and to dust I will return. I get a view something like an astronaut on his way to the moon who looks back and sees the earth in relation to its environment. I see myself and my world as microcosm in relation to the vastness of God's infinite macrocosm. But, unlike the atheist, I am not crushed by such a sight. I do not despair that I am less than a speck on the windowpane of time and space. For God has assured me that I am precious to him in spite of my apparent lack of importance in his cosmos. I am called to be his heir, with a unique purpose in his plan, to be mature, no longer a child blown about by careless winds.

Therefore, as I stand in my own place in time and look back, I see the footsteps of many others as well. I see the foundation built by God through the saints of every generation, carefully planned to lead me step by step along his way. And I see ahead the opportunities of finding more treasures, of seeking out new riches, of growing more in his grace and love.

And what does that mean for the present? Is it merely a pause between two worlds without a meaning of its own? I don't believe so. Whether we take the present moment for reflection or activity, the present is what we have at our disposal to live. It is the "bird in the hand," the only segment of time we have to employ. My moments looking back can be worthwhile if they are not spent in dreaming of what might have been. My looks into the future must be more than wishful "if-onlys." My moments today must have meaning in relation to my past and my future and must also be used in the very best way as my immediate opportunity, my *now* with God and his world.

> Trust no Future, howe'er pleasant!
>   Let the dead Past bury its dead!
> Act—act in the living present!
>   Heart within, and God o'erhead! [11]

HENRY WADSWORTH LONGFELLOW

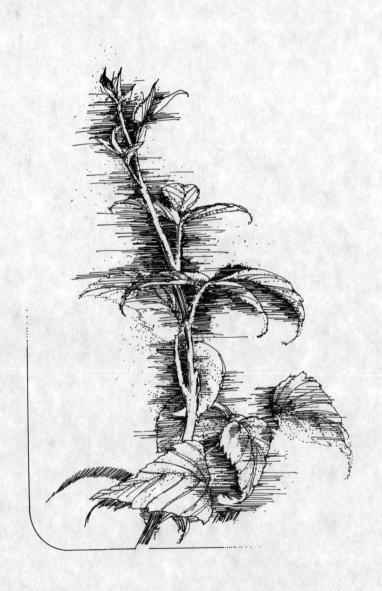

The "great" commitment
is so much easier
than the ordinary everyday one —
and can all too easily
shut our hearts to the latter. [12]

DAG HAMMARSKJÖLD

8. ONE MORE MOUNTAIN

I must stop here to make something clear. I fear I might be giving the impression that my times in the berry patch, after the initial adjustment, were full of mystic inspiration. That isn't exactly how it was. Berry picking is tedious, frustrating work. There were discomforts and inconveniences to be endured. The lessons I learned were hard won, if not in tears, at least in sweat and some minor scratches. Those hours were not just a "bowl of berries."

I have just finished reading another in a long line of books describing someone's personal encounter with God and the results in the author's life. Some of those books are shallow and superficial; some, like the one I recently finished reading, are well written and real. But even this one shared one failing with the others. It concentrated on the miraculous. It described only the mountaintops. As I read this man's story I learned to like him, and I wanted to know him, not only through the pages of religious rhetoric, but as a friend. I wanted to know how he worked out his newfound faith in daily things. Life, even on the highest plane, is not a bowl of berries either. I have my mountaintops, too, but I don't take giant strides from one of them to the other. I get to them by marching, step by step through the valleys in between.

I got my pailful of berries the same way, one at a time. On one particularly fruitless trip to pick blueberries with my sister-in-law, she commented that she was glad we didn't have to feed our families on our harvest. The discouragements of daily-ness are greater foes of the spirit than the seduction to scarlet sins. We get worn down and worn out by them. They tangle us in their web of self-concern. We suffer from the "tyranny of the urgent."

Of course, no one would write a book describing her daily struggle with the laundry or the subway or the neighbor's gossip. It would be dull and depressing. But a glimpse of such plodding amidst the drama gives me a place to get a handhold on the climb up the mountain. Bruce Larson, for instance, confesses (in *Dare to Live Now*) that his conversion didn't cure him of his distaste for taking out the garbage. Keith Miller (in *Taste of New Wine*) admits he struck out in his first attempts at integrating his new faith into his family life. These secrets shared are a source of hope for me. Not because I like to see others defeated in their attempts at victorious living, but because I know that I am not alone in my faltering. Paul Tournier, the renowned Swiss psychologist and theologian, says that the day he sat down and shared his own problem with a patient was a new beginning for him. He realized that counseling is a two-way street. As long as the patient sees his counselor as someone different, someone who has not experienced or fallen prey to the same anxieties, there is no opportunity for dialogue. But when that person can see the counselor as a fellow struggler who has worked through some of his problems, the sigh of relief is like a mighty wind that carries away a good measure of guilt and frustration.

And for us all, there is one Counselor who has experienced our humanness without stumbling. It is to him we go together for the healing of our bruised egos and scratched superficiality. It is with him alone that we can open ourselves in complete honesty, hiding nothing. It is his hand that leads through the tedious, tormenting valleys, through steaming jungles of tangled thought, over the dry, trackless deserts of boredom, through the swift currents of adversity and trial.

And when we falter and fall, when we get bogged down in the quicksand of minute-by-minute living and say, "I'll never make it," he is there to renew our strength and vision and encourage us to go on. Then, when we get to that mountain eyrie together and we look longingly at the eagle whose wings carry him so easily from peak to peak, we hear the Counselor's promise, "Because I am with you, the next climb will be easier, the next valley not quite so dark." Hallelujah!

> Ever' man wants life to be a fine thing, and a easy. 'Tis fine, . . . powerful fine, but 'tain't easy.[13]
>
> JODY'S FATHER

*The Son of Man has come
to search out and save
what is lost.*[14]

JESUS

9. THE ONE LOST

If I were presumptuous enough to update one of our Lord's parables, I think it would be the one about the woman who swept her house clean to find the coin that she lost. Inflation has devalued the coin, any coin, so much that few of us would go to so much trouble for it. On the other hand, I know what he meant about the one lost sheep, even though I've had nothing to do with sheep. Sheep are valuable, not only because of the current cost of meat, but because they have a uniqueness. Coins are impersonal objects; sheep are, at least to the shepherd, individual creatures he comes to recognize and know. I might go out and look for one lost sheep.

It might surprise you to know that the same concept applies to raspberries. If that seems absurd, remember what I said about my perspective in that kingdom. It is like walking through C. S. Lewis's closet and coming out in Narnia. I don't mean that raspberries have personalities or that I can recognize one from another when I pour out my pail, but they do have about them a uniqueness, an importance, that you can't realize when you pick up the box in the supermarket.

I have spent precious minutes combing the underbrush for a berry that slipped through my fingers and dropped to the tangle underneath my feet. It happened often to the largest, juiciest ones because they were so perfectly ripe they seemed eager to be picked and fell at the slightest touch. I have climbed through gnarled trees and canes to reach one or two very special berries that were too enticing to pass up. Because there is no way to pick raspberries wholesale, each one is noticed and appreciated as it falls with a gentle plop into my pail.

Even on a good day, when my pail was filled with relative ease, I would mourn over any that were lost or that I could not reach. My values in the raspberry patch were such that I could not afford to lose one, no matter how many I had.

That must be how the Lord feels about his children. He never reaches the point where he says, "I don't need that one," or, "This one is not worth the trouble." The one lost one is worth all the effort it requires to go after him or her; the one who will not be reached grieves his heart, no matter how many others have said yes to him. There is no point at which he gives up.

In *The Great Divorce*, C. S. Lewis illustrates the supreme effort by the redeemed on behalf of the lost ones. They put off their own journey to glory in order to come back and help others on the way, exposing themselves once again to the pettiness of carnal humans. But, although they are willing to make this sacrifice, they cannot make the decision for the lost. "Aye, there's the rub," says Hamlet. If only parents or

pastors or great spiritual giants could choose God for
others, how much easier it would be! But, in spite of
the yearning heart of God that stretches forth in love to
give us more than we could ever think to ask, we, like
Lewis's ghosts and the melancholy Hamlet, chose the
insufficiency of the known in place of the risky
potential of the unknown. Lewis's graphic description
of this process points to the source of the problem:
while the redeemed one stands by encouraging,
reaching out, doing everything but carrying the lost one
bodily beyond himself, that pitiful one dwells so
intently on his suspicion, fear, and his own ego that he
gradually shrivels, fades, and fizzles into nothingness.

There were times when my own discomfort or the
tangle of brush loomed larger than the promise of
exquisite fruit. I can't claim to have given my utmost
for every last berry in the patch. But while I was there,
I did exert effort that, on my normal value scale,
seemed unreasonable. If a berry was hidden under a
broad leaf or behind an impassable thicket, it was the
obstacle that prevented me from getting it, not my own
arbitrary choice of good over bad, best over better. I
wanted them all. I didn't want to lose even one. I am
sorry for every one I missed, not because of greed or
hunger, but because of lost potential and missed
opportunity.

> Faith would be that God is self-limited utterly by
> his creation—a contraction of the scope of his
> will; that he bound himself to time and its hazards
> and haps as a man would lash himself to a tree for love.[15]
>   ANNIE DILLARD

*The counterfeit of obedience
is a state of mind in which
you work up occasions
to sacrifice yourself. . . .
It is a great deal better
to fulfil the purpose
of God in your life
by discerning His will
than to perform great acts
of self-sacrifice.* [16]

OSWALD CHAMBERS

10. HOW MUCH IS ENOUGH?

I hadn't made many trips into the berry patch before I discovered the trick to finding good fruit. It was not in looking for healthy canes, but for the brightness of the berries. Often the most enticing fruit was found on canes so dry and barren they looked scarcely alive.

At first I was excited at the obvious illustration. There was an appealing nobility in the picture of the bush burning itself up for the sake of the fruit. It recalled not only the bloody sacrifices in the coliseum, but all the unrecorded and unheralded martyrs of God throughout the centuries. I was reminded that sometimes, in order for one to live, another one must die.

But the Holy Spirit wasn't accompanying me on my early morning trips to point up the obvious. Something else nagged at me. What did that universal truth have to do with me? I was not going about burning myself up for anything or anyone. I remembered the sentimental stories I had heard about mothers who shivered through winters with no coats in order to provide piano lessons for their children. I thought of my own parents and the things I know they must have gone without to make life easier for us. I didn't stack up very well against such examples. The guilt pang stung like the nettles I brushed against. Is that, I asked myself and my Companion, the only way to bear fruit? To give up everything? (Jesus said it, didn't he?) If so, I wasn't going to make it.

I thought of my comfortable home with its do-everything appliances, the closet full of clothes, the cupboards and freezer full of convenience foods. The thorns scratched deeper as I considered the cosmetics in the bathroom drawer, the soaps and lotions that required time to use in grooming my imperfect self. Not nearly so much as others, I argued, not nearly so much. But was even that too much? Did it mean that my "fruit" would suffer? Was I putting too much effort into the care of the cane and not enough into the production of the fruit?

My first thoughts went to my children. I have seen mothers at Scouts and PTA who seem almost unaware of themselves as persons, so intent are they on their bright, cultivated children. In contrast, mine sometimes look, as one woman put it, "like the kind I wouldn't want my kids to play with." Not neglected, but not fussed over. We have had a good life together, and I'm not sure it could have been much better if I had played the "professional" mother part. I admire some women who do, but for me it would be just that—playing a part, acting out the drama as someone else. I often worry that I should be doing more, but it puts great stain on my existential view to see my worth as relative only to my sacrifice on their behalf. If that

pattern evolves from one person living only for another
and that one for another, where does the worth of any
one person come into being? Are we to snatch little
pieces of individual worth as we go along, like
collecting crumbs from the master's table?

I came up against the same dilemma when I thought
about my husband. I have considered the possibility
(not very seriously, but I have considered it) of living in
his shadow, tuning my whole life to his key. I
considered it because I wondered if I could help him
most that way, if the less I became, the greater he
would be. But I couldn't accept that because I know he
prefers relating to a person, not a mindless puppet.

So where does all that take me in my search for an
answer to the burnt up bush? Do all the midnight
feedings and toilet scrubbings and birthday cakes and
lonesome weeks left alone at home count? May I add
the aching arms and wet laps and chapped hands and
stretch marks? Is there a scale or a point system or some
absolute common denominator that I can use to
measure myself against God's standard?

As I asked those questions, I kept coming up against
Jesus' standards. He pushed aside the excesses of point
systems and score keeping. In their place he proclaimed
standards that are even more difficult because they force
us into questions (the kind I was asking) and situation
decisions. He didn't give blanket laws for the masses
but laws tailored to fit individuals. Through them he
takes me out of the rare mountain atmosphere of
"spirituality" and leads me through the valleys of

reality. There he reveals me to myself and shows me also what I am able, through him, to become. He speaks to me in the small sign over the kitchen door that says "Willing servant" (help me to do my tasks willingly and lovingly). His law is paraphrased by a Catholic priest, "What matters most in the apostolate is a willingness to be used, rather than the inner conviction that we have something to contribute (keep me from being led away from your purpose for me)." My Lord warns me about "cheap grace" through his servants Luther and Bonhoeffer and reminds me through his friend Karl Olsson that the biggest ego trip in the world is to deny the ego.

I know that I was created in God's image, destined to be his child in the highest sense. I know that sin has distorted that image and crippled my ability to be like him. But I know also that I am expected to attain a measure of wholeness in this life and to serve him in a unique way. That way will not be my mother's way or your way because he cares enough about each of us not to force us into sameness. It is in following him into that way that we are fulfilled and can end our days on earth, whether withered or green, with the affirmation, "It is finished."

> For that is what is meant by *caritas*: it is the freedom which follows upon the capacity to experience as joy what you are given to do.[17]

THOMAS HOWARD

Haste is not always speed.
We must learn to work and wait.
This is like God, who perfects his works
through beautiful gradations.

AUTHOR UNKNOWN

11. THE TURTLE PACE

In the berry patch I was forced to work at turtle speed. There was no way for me to whiz through it in high gear. But once I became accustomed to the environment, I liked working that way. It eased the aches of super-speed living in the other world. It was balm for nerves rubbed raw by irritating pressures and demands. It reawakened in me the childlike ability to stop and notice details.

I concluded that I needed a berry patch throughout the year. Not a literal one, but a refuge of some kind in my own time and space environment where I could feel the same sense of removal from the whirling world. If you have reached middle age, as I had, following the ethic of efficiency and diligence, if you were raised on the "work now, play later" philosophy, and if your conscience has been conditioned to think that all the good works in the world are there waiting for you to take care of, you know how difficult it is to break the pattern and run any part of the race as a turtle.

But I am convinced that each of us needs to break the pace from time to time, and do just that. Not only for health, but for fulfillment. Even the Lord rested after his creative splurge, and he ordained a day of rest for us as well. You have no doubt heard of famous men like J. C. Penney who, after enduring the slavery of compulsive fortune making, realized that nothing had value if there was no time for reflection and enjoyment. But that lesson is not only for tycoons. It is also for housewives and mechanics, for secretaries and farmers.

There is no set rule for the turtle walk—when or where or how. We, each of us, must decide for ourselves what suits us best. My time alone in the berry patch taught me one thing, however. Our "rest," what we choose to do in slow motion, must be far enough removed from our usual pace that we are not tempted to speed up. Depending on your circumstances, that may be a physical removal or a mental one. A homemaker may need to get away from the constant demands of her home in order to slow her time clock. The businessman may use his time on the rush hour speedway in the morning and evening, not to slow his car, but his thoughts, winding down from a pressure-cooker day.

These times need not be long, and they can be "stolen" from the part of your life that will cause your conscience the least anguish. I spend a few moments of quiet with the sunrise and dedicate my Sunday afternoons to reading or writing or walking, all at a less urgent pace. And I have found that this is not time lost. It has such a calming, healing effect that it touches the more hectic hours as well. It creeps like verdant ivy to "green up" the parched wasteland of my mind and pours soothing ointment over tense anxiety, softening the harsh edges of life.

In the woods I heard the aria of one bird in command performance for me. I saw tiny bits of moss clinging to life on a rotting log. I eavesdropped on the whispering leaves' conversations and studied the magnificent perfection of a spider's web that no other human had seen. Cars speeding past me in clouds of dust saw nothing but a green blur. Hikers on the road saw no more than a mass of tangled leaves. I alone, in the solitude of that place, was seeing and discovering the riches it held—not because I was any worthier or because my vision was better or my perception more acute, but simply because I slowed down and walked with the turtle.

It's not easy to be a turtle today, but it's harder, in the long run, to be a hare. The berries I took out of the patch were eaten with relish but were gone in a few hours. The harvest of peace and aroused sensitivity is not so quickly lost. It is a part of the great harvest of Truth, a taste of the living water that quenches the thirst of my soul.

Each morning the child cups his hands and receives life, thumb-rim full, and lets fear slip through his little fingers.[18]

EDNA HONG

I shall be telling this with a sigh
Somewhere ages and ages hence:
Two roads diverged in a wood, and I —
I took the one less traveled by,
And that has made all the difference. [19]

ROBERT FROST

12. THE NARROW ROAD

After two years of picking berries in the patch across from our cabin, I was told that there was another place down the road that was even better—and easier. I'm not sure if it was the "better" or the "easier" that tempted me; perhaps I was just ready for a change. I decided to try it.

Unlike our patch, this one was below the road, alongside a swampy area and away from the tall trees of the woods. It was quite open and free of the hazards of my other place. I expected to move through quickly and fill my pail with ease but I was disappointed. There were signs that other pickers had been there recently and whether because of their efficient harvest or my informant's exaggeration, the pickings were not what I expected.

It was disappointing in another way, too. I had come to expect more than berries from my excursions. Once I plunged into the depth of bushes and trees, I entered into that other world where time slowed down and values turned topsy-turvy. My thoughts kept pace with the lazy hum of insects instead of the raucous noise of the radio. Sounds of the outside world were muffled and unreal; they didn't touch me in my sanctuary.

This new place was different. I was no closer in distance to the road, but without the shield of enveloping brush, I was not at all removed. Every car that drove by violated my solitude. My concentration was easily broken because there was so little that needed concentration. In my own patch, it took all my attention to work my way through the thicket, to find the fruit, and to avoid the impediments. Here there was no such challenge. While the fruit was not so abundant as I had anticipated, it was easy to find and no trouble to reach. Only occasionally did I have to strain to get what I wanted, and much of the walking cost little more than would a stroll through the park. It wasn't much fun at all.

Perhaps if I had returned to that place again, I would have found rewards there, too. I remember that my first time in our own patch was less than I expected. But I didn't go back. The challenge of my own patch had more to offer. All the difficulties and irritations of that place now made it more worthwhile. I am by nature quite lazy. If I had found the easy patch first, I'm sure I would have continued picking there and avoided the more difficult one altogether. I would have been satisfied with the lesser of the two because I wouldn't have known that difference. It may be like thinking that "store bought" cookies are good until you taste something homemade. If you have been raised on homemade, the cardboard facsimiles, even those made by elves, can never measure up. And homemade is worth the trouble, at least once in awhile, because of that difference.

So it was with increased excitement that I returned to my own familiar ground the following day. I could understand then why Jesus talked about the "narrow Way." I grew up from my Sunday school concept of it as a restriction from anything that was fun. I saw it instead as a path directed toward a goal, with much to enjoy along the way. It was a protection from outside influences that could mar the excitement and joy of the path itself. It was a road on which I was free to follow the leading in its own context, undeterred by distractions that would lure me away. It wasn't only the distinction between easy and difficult; it was in being set apart for a purpose.

I don't know if Frost's "less traveled road" and Jesus' "narrow Way" are the same. But they do both assume that the wide, easy road of "everybody's doing it" has its own rewards and that those rewards lack the one thing needful. When the traveler chooses the less trampled, narrow path, following his Leader in ultimate trust, it "makes all the difference."

> Go in through the narrow gate, for the gate is wide and the road is easy that leads to hell, and there are many who travel it. The gate is narrow and the way is hard that leads to life, and few people find it. [20]
>
> JESUS

*It does not take much strength
to do things, but it requires great strength
to decide on what to do.*

ELBERT HUBBARD

13. DECISIONS, DECISIONS

One of the beauties of picking raspberries was the
freedom of choice I had once I was within my world
behind the bushes. Depending on my mood, I would
wander aimlessly through the brush or I could be more
methodical and plot a strategy as I went through the
harvesting rite. On more energetic days I might work
twice as long and twice as hard as on days when only a
craving for fruit was able to lure me away from my book
and the rocking chair.

But most often, even on my wandering days, there
were times as I picked when I had to make a decision.
Which way to go? Should I try for the canes ahead
where I could see one or two brightly tempting berries,
or go back for the ones I had missed behind me? Should
I stay near the road or go farther back into the brush?
And, eventually, there was the decision of whether to
stop or go on for another few minutes. The choice was
usually made without serious contemplation.
Nevertheless, a choice was made. Moving my feet in
one direction rather than another was a decision.

I am not an able choice maker. I would much rather
leave most decisions to others. Those which are mine
alone to make—what to fix for dinner, which day

would be best for grocery shopping—are difficult. I went shopping with a friend once and was filled with admiration when she chose two rooms full of furniture after walking through just *one* store *one* time! Another time she and I went shoe shopping, and she picked out two pair before I had even decided which ones to try on. Decision making was definitely one of her strong points.

My tactic so often is "not deciding." I can't make up my mind, so I don't do anything. If I don't get around to calling for tickets for the symphony or the Ice Follies, we don't go. If I stall getting my hair cut or the carpet shampooed, my hair gets longer and the rug gets dirtier. It is easy to excuse such lack of action with, "I couldn't decide," but the truth is I did decide. I decided just as surely as if I had said, "I won't," because my lack of action had consequences just as my action would have.

Jesus pointed to this truth when he said, "He who is not for me is against me." It must be one way or the other. Time and life do not stand still when we can't make up our minds. My hair doesn't stop growing, and the symphony and Follies go on without me. God gives us every opportunity to say "aye" or "nay," to declare ourselves for him or against him, but time does not stand still until we do. Life goes on and is affected by our decision in a thousand ways.

There is a great emphasis on deciding for Christ in order to get to heaven or to escape hell (one is more important than the other to different people). But that decision also affects our lives here and now. My decisions in the berry patch had much less impact on my yield of berry-in-the-pail than on the work at hand. Choosing one way might mean having to tackle the obstacles of fallen trees or determined bees. My ultimate concern was to attain the riches of a pail full of fruit, but the choices I made determined the conditions under which I would get that fruit.

I have moments of thrilling anticipation when I read John's glorious ode describing heavenly choirs echoing the refrain of nature in praises to the Lord of lords (Rev. 19:1-8). But I thrill, also, to the quiet voice of that same Lord who comes to me each day saying, "Father, forgive them . . ." and who raises me from my cot of futility with the simple words, "Rise up and walk." My decision means more than some far-off promise of tomorrow. Eternity is *now*, and my choice determines how I will live that *now*, with the Lord or without him. That is one choice I have no trouble making. I am his!

> I don't know Who—or what—put the question, I don't know when it was put. I don't even remember answering. But at some moment I did answer *Yes* to Someone—or Something—and from that hour I was certain that existence is meaningful and that, therefore, my life, in self-surrender, had a goal.[21]
>
> DAG HAMMARSKJÖLD

It took so long to bake it,
And I'll never have the
recipe again. [22]

JIM WEBB

14. LAST CHAPTER

After a two years' absence from the lake, I returned hungry for both the fruit and the labor of the raspberry patch. The first few days were too hot and too busy with work on the cabin. When a day finally came that promised to be cooler, I forced myself out of bed before the rest of the family, donned my protective clothing, sprayed myself liberally with mosquito repellent, and plunged into the brush.

The mosquitoes were delighted to find fresh nourishment in their territory and seemed unaware of the claims made by repellent manufacturers. The brush had grown back two or threefold from earlier tramplings and the rotten logs had become rottener. While the bugs bit and the vines untied my shoelaces, I fought my way through the alien tangle on the promise of a slim harvest and some intangible metaphysical rewards. I lasted less than one hour.

When I returned to the cabin my pail was only slightly heavier than when I had left. Worse than that, I had been miserable the whole time I worked. There were times, in passing remembered spots, that I tried to ignore the discomfort and concentrate on generating some deep, significant idea, but it was no good. I began to suspect that, although I might go picking again, the days of inspiration in the raspberry patch were over.

Later that evening, in dialogue with friends, we discussed goals and vocations. A wise young man shared his views.

"I know that what I am doing right now is right for me at this time, but I'm not projecting a plan for myself beyond it. I am certain it will not be a permanent arrangement. If the Lord of the universe has a place for me in his plan, then I must be available to be used in that plan in his way and not set myself an objective that I confuse with his plan."

This man was doing something he was good at, something he was trained for, and something he enjoyed. But he was not so immersed in all of that that he was not open to another call. "For everything there is a season. . . ."

I guessed then that the Lord of the universe might have another raspberry patch for me to work in. He had taught me lessons in the woods that I could translate into meaning, but he did not intend for me to lean on those experiences forever. To expect learning always to come from the same environment is too great a crutch for one who has heard the Master say, "Follow me."

One of the difficulties in growing up, for both adolescent and adult, is the necessity for letting go. The reluctance to grow out of immature relationships, to move on to the challenge of life's real problems, to mature beyond the need for someone else's dependence

on us, to give up the familiar securities—all require a
wrenching separation that is accompanied by a
poignant sense of loss. Jesus was continually requiring
this of people he met. He accepted people where they
were, healed them right there, and then set for them
goals that put them on a new path.

"Go and sin no more," to someone whose life had
been controlled by sin.

"Tell no man," to the experience-oriented gossip.

"Go and tell," to the inarticulate fisherman.

To the letter-of-the-law abiders he uncovered the
real law, to those abused by the letter of the law, he
proclaimed mercy. Jesus was the true revealer, but he
was not the revealer of static, ironclad truth as
understood by traditional dogmatism. It was not the
truth of the "comfortable pew" or the "we've always
done it this way" doctrine. It was truth in
flux—challenging, moving, pushing, pressing.
Someone once noted that if reading the Bible makes us
feel comfortable, we are reading it wrong.

Not too long ago we were looking at old slides of the
family. As I watched the series of pictures of chubby
babies, I could almost feel the downy softness of new
hair and the grip of tiny fingers on mine. There was a
faint longing to hold those little bodies again, to be
involved in new teeth and faltering first steps. I guess I
will always feel that tender nostalgia mingled with some
regret that I did not appreciate it enough at the time it
was happening. But, if I learned anything from the
raspberry patch, it is that I cannot live in that past or

in any other past. When one experience or function has fulfilled itself for me, then I can move on with great expectations for another. To me, Jesus' promise of "many mansions" is not an invitation for heavenly harp playing but for here-and-now living. He has prepared a wonderful home for me to explore, a ladder with a variety of rungs, a smorgasbord of experiences, if only I have eyes to see and ears to hear.

> He who binds to himself a joy
> Does the winged life destroy;
> But he who kisses the joy as it flies
> Lives in eternity's sunrise. [23]

WILLIAM BLAKE

Reflection

In the cool of morning, I cross the road,
climbing the bank
toward the raspberry canes.
A sentinel bird
chides me for invading his home,
gossiping to his neighbors
about my bad manners.

I am now in a world apart,
my own world,
where no other human voice or presence
shares these moments with me.
I am a giant in this world,
dwarfed only by the trees above me.
But I am not empowered by my greater size,
for I am an alien, a stranger.

Familiar comfort left behind
on the other side of the road,
I seek identity with this new world
and what it offers—
the chirp of a shy bird
flitting across my path,
the hum of mosquitoes,

the drone of bees,
the cool, velvet feel of berries
on my fingertips,
the soft sound
of their fall into my pail.
I walk hesitatingly over rotting logs
green with moss
and tred lightly on soft beds of needles
and old leaves,
careful not to bruise the ferns.
Thistles guard the choicest fruit,
or sometimes bees.
I do not challenge them.

The sun moves higher
and my jacket is uncomfortable.
The birches cease their ballet.
A stillness settles over all,
broken by the sound of distant thunder
and the sudden roar of a boat's engine,
ripping the silence to pieces,
leaving a ragged edged echo.
The spell is broken.
It is time to go home.

NOTES

1. From "Aurora Leigh," book vii.
2. *The Divine Yes* (Nashville: Abingdon, 1975), pp. 53-54.
3. *My Utmost for His Highest* (New York: Dodd, Mead & Co., 1935), p. 95.
4. *The Velveteen Rabbit* (New York: Doubleday, 1958), pp. 17, 20.
5. From "In No Strange Land," *The Kingdom of God.*
6. *Death Comes for the Archbishop* (New York: Vintage, 1971), p. 50.
7. *North Star Country* (New York: Duell, Sloan & Pearce, 1945), p. 185.
8. *Julius Caesar,* act 4, sc. 3, lines 217-220.
9. *The Cost of Discipleship* (London: SCM Press Ltd., 1959), p. 41.
10. *The Cost of Discipleship,* p. 89.
11. From "A Psalm of Life."
12. *Markings,* trans. Leif Sjöberg and W. H. Auden (New York: Alfred A. Knopf, 1966), p. 131.
13. Marjorie Kinnan Rawlings, *The Yearling* (New York: Charles Scribner's Sons, 1966), p. 403.
14. Luke 19:10 (New American Bible).
15. *Holy the Firm* (New York: Harper & Row, 1977), p. 47.
16. *My Utmost for His Highest,* p. 160.
17. *Christ the Tiger* (Philadelphia: Lippincott, 1967), p. 157.
18. *Clues to the Kingdom* (Minneapolis: Augsburg, 1968), p. 46.
19. From "The Road Not Taken."
20. Matthew 7:13-14 (*Good News for Modern Man*).
21. *Markings,* p. 205.
22. From the song "MacArthur Park."
23. From "Auguries of Innocence."